Knowing the God of Compassion

Knowing the God of Compassion

Spirituality and Persons
Living with AIDS

Richard P. Hardy

NOVALIS

To Hiro
He loved.
He was loved.

Cover art: "Living Flame of Love" by Marcel Morin
Layout and design: Gilles Lépine
Scripture quotations are from the *New Revised Standard Version*
© 1993 Novalis, Saint Paul University, Ottawa
Editorial office: Novalis, Saint Paul University, 223 Main Street,
Ottawa, Ontario K1S 1C4. Business office: Novalis, 49 Front Street East,
2nd Floor, Toronto, Ontario M5E 1B3
Printed in Canada

Canadian Cataloguing in Publication Data

Hardy, Richard P.
  Knowing the God of compassion: spirituality
and persons living with AIDS

(Inner journey series)
Includes bibliographical references.
ISBN 2-89088-632-8

  1. AIDS (Disease) — Patients — Religious Life.
2. AIDS (Disease) — Religious aspects —
Christianity. I. Title. II. Series.

RC607.A26K66 1993   216.8'321969792   C93-090530-X

NOVALIS

Contents

Introduction

Over the past five years, I have been gifted to know and journey with several persons living with AIDS. All were gay men. Some were former students. Some were friends. But all of them gave me something that no one and nothing else could give — a deeper experience of what it means to be fully human in a world that so desperately needs to know this. They also taught me what it means to believe in a loving, compassionate God. They were men who had struggled with life.

Our churches and our society had oppressed and marginalized these men. They often felt rejected, experienced great pain and sensed a reciprocal anger burning within them. But this gave them an opportunity to move through rejection and loss to transformation. And they dared to let go and to live their part of the human journey as authentically as they possibly could. They had not chosen to be gay. They were gay, purely and simply. Society had told them in a variety of ways from the day of their birth that they might be gay. But they were told to be inauthentic, to hide what they were and to deny who they were. Most tried to do this. They had to; how else could they survive? They did not want to be like others who, finding life intolerable, committed suicide. Living "in the closet" seemed to be their only option. Or was it? With all the courage they could muster, they gradually realized that living the lie was itself a lie. If they were to be fully the ones God had gifted them to be, they had to be themselves, even if others — and perhaps those they loved most deeply — could not accept it.

Some of the people I refer to in this book I have known personally. Others I know only through what they have written about their experience of living with AIDS. Most of what follows is really theirs — the narration of their experience, the affirmation of their being. This is the story of people claiming the gift of their God-given selves.

Because of them I decided to write this book. I want you to know what marvellous persons they are. They have been graced by our loving God . (I am not implying that God gave them AIDS. God did not. But they were graced because God dared to remain and suffer and *live* with them.) They neither chose to have AIDS nor to be infected by the Human Immuno-deficiency Virus (HIV). It happened. And in their journey in life, they discovered the God of compassion made known to us in Jesus Christ. They came to see and experience in their very lives the love this compassionate God has, and always has had, for them. In the process, they discovered that this love enabled them to love others more deeply and to serve them and be with them in their times of pain, anguish and hopelessness. In short, they became the touch of God for others. And in that very being for others, they found themselves gifted with new life in a variety of ways.

So, I am writing this book for them. I believe their spirituality and their lives need to be known so that we can all grow more deeply human. The spirituality in this book comes from them. And this is the only true spirituality — one which stems from the believer's lived experience here and now with God. I mentioned above that, for the most part, the voices in this book are those of gay men living with AIDS. Consequently their spirituality has a certain colouring because of the oppression they had to endure even before they found themselves living with HIV or AIDS. But I believe their spirituality is one which all men and women, regardless of sexual orientation, will find life-giving.

Their stories and my reflections cannot cover the whole gamut of human experience. There are other stories. There are other paths. I think of the women who are seropositive or live with AIDS. For way too long, they were left out of the picture because the symptoms which defined AIDS were those of males. They also had to struggle with a medical establishment that often did not always take seriously illnesses which afflict the female population. I think of their suffering when they realize that they may never be able to have children again — or at all. I think of their utter despair as they wonder what will happen to their children — some of whom may be HIV positive or living with AIDS. What of the children who at twelve or fourteen have the responsibility of caring for dying parents or for their younger siblings thrust upon them? I think of the mother in her eighties whose only remaining child dies suddenly from an AIDS-related cancer. Her already failing mind courageously tries to cope with something she simply doesn't understand. Who is there to help her? Clearly, some people are affected more intensely than others. All suffer greatly, but some more than others.

Some seem to have no quiet paths. Some seem to have no success. Yet, they are no less real and valuable to themselves and to others; and their stories and their lives are important. Would that everyone could hear their stories! Someday, perhaps, we will realize that each and every human being has a unique story that is a treasure for all. Then we will be one human community.

This book is an opportunity for people living with HIV and AIDS to tell their story and to let their spirituality unfurl before you. But I also have another reason for writing: too many families, partners, friends and others suffer from the stigma society imposes upon their partner, son or daughter, or friend. I want them to realize this stigma is unjust and unfair. Shame should not characterize the life of a person living with this disease: AIDS is a disease, not a social commentary.

I would like to thank Dr. Kenneth Russell of Saint Paul University for his suggestions about style and for his reflections on my reflections. My editor, Michael O'Hearn of Novalis, helped me make this book accessible in so many ways. However, I take full responsibility for the ideas expressed herein. As well, I am indebted to Ottawa physician Bruce R. Marshall, MD, and Dr. John R. Williams of Ottawa for assisting me with the section on the medical facts about AIDS.

And I wish to offer a very special thank you to all the persons living with AIDS who shared their experiences personally or through books or conferences.

I would like to add one final note. With the exception of the Reverend Ronald Bergeron, the former pastor of the Metropolitan Community Church in Ottawa, the names of the people I speak of have been changed and the details of their circumstances fictionalized. I do this to protect their privacy as they continue to enrich us with the gift of who they are. I hope this approach will be unnecessary some day. When that day arrives, the human community will have understood what it means to be truly human and, therefore, truly Christian.

The Body of Christ has AIDS. Whether you are HIV positive, have AIDS, or know someone who is or has, all of us people of God, be we gay or straight, men or women, are living with AIDS. This is your story. It is my story. It is our story.

Richard P. Hardy
Ottawa, Ontario
24 July 1993

1

AIDS and
spirituality

American physicians were rather taken
aback in 1981 when they first discovered a rare form of skin
cancer (Kaposi's Sarcoma, or KS) and of pneumonia (Pneumocystis Carinii Pneumonia, or PCP) in young gay men. Soon
they found that intravenous drug users suffered from the same
problems. By 1982 the first cases were seen in Canada. The
origins and causes were unknown. In 1984, researchers in
France isolated a retrovirus. Eventually called the Human
Immunodeficiency Virus (HIV), it attacked many types of cells,
especially the immune system's CD4 cells. HIV destroyed these
cells and left the person open to infection by various opportun-
istic diseases. While HIV seems to be the primary viral agent
responsible for AIDS, other factors have not been ruled out as
possible causes. Genetic make-up, personality, sexual activity
backgrounds, a history of immuno-suppressing diseases (such
as tuberculosis and various sexually transmitted diseases), alco-
hol consumption and smoking may all have a causal role to
play.

Studies have shown that HIV cannot be transmitted casually. There is no danger in touching, hugging or kissing a person who is infected by HIV. Nor can the virus be transmitted by eating and drinking from the same utensils as used by persons who are HIV positive. HIV is spread through a direct exchange of infected bodily fluids, specifically blood, semen and vaginal secretions. Infection occurs when HIV enters into the bloodstream. Before a test for the HIV antibodies was developed and marketed in 1985, some blood used for transfusions and the making of blood products for hemophiliacs had been contaminated. Hence, some hemophiliacs and other persons who needed blood transfusions were infected with the virus. Presently, all donated blood is tested. Blood products are also treated to assure the killing of the virus, and are now safe.

HIV is transmitted primarily through unsafe sexual activity and the sharing of unclean needles among drug users. Infected pregnant women can transmit the virus to their unborn children; however, not all children born to infected mothers develop the virus. (The percentage of such children developing the virus is between 16 and 30% in the United States.) Medical literature suggests that infected mothers may pass the virus to their children through breast-feeding.

HIV can remain inactive within the infected person for periods of months and even years. During this time the person will experience no symptoms. Once the virus becomes active, however, it gradually destroys particular kinds of white blood cells called T4 cells (or T-Helper cells). This generally happens at a rate which causes a decrease in the T4 cell count (cells/mm^3) of about 100 cells per year. (The "normal" range for T4 cells is anywhere from 600-1400 cells /mm^3). The destruction of T-Helper cells severely restricts the immune system's ability to respond to infection. Early testing can permit early treatment should a person be found to have HIV antibodies. In this and other ways, the disease is becoming better managed. At the present time, various drugs are available for treatment, such as

Azidothymidine (AZT) alone or in combination with others, such as Dideoxyinosine (DDI) or Dideoxycytidine (DDC). These inhibit the virus and slow its progressive destruction of the T4 cells. But they are not a cure. Most doctors still recommend the use of AZT once the T4 cell count is below 500, despite recent findings in European research that suggest that AZT is not as helpful as formerly thought. Once the blood count falls below 200, a preventative treatment for PCP is usually begun.

As the virus weakens and gradually destroys the immune system, the person falls prey to a variety of diseases — diseases with which a normally healthy immune system can easily deal. Among these diseases are KS, PCP, oral and esophageal thrush in men, and aggressive and recurrent vaginal yeast infection and cervical cancer in women. Often there is a wasting away of tissue, leaving the individual weak, very thin and looking much older in appearance. Other diseases which can develop include toxoplasmosis, which affects the brain, and cryptococal infection, caused by a fungus affecting the brain and other parts of the body; mycobacterial disease, which can produce tuberculosis or other problems in various parts of the body; various fungal infections, assorted viral infections including cytomegolavirus (CMV), which causes retinitis and various gastrointestinal diseases; and several other malignancies. Once any of these are diagnosed, the person is said to have AIDS.[1] People with AIDS are beginning to live longer because of early medical treatment. Consequently, more of them are experiencing dementia (serious emotional and mental deterioration) because of infections involving the brain, most commonly by the HIV itself.

AIDS has caused the deaths of hundreds of thousands of people throughout the world, and the rate of infection continues to climb. Every 14 seconds someone in the world is

---

1. As of January 1, 1993, the Center for Disease Control in Atlanta included female symptoms in their definition of AIDS. Until then, the AIDS-defining symptoms were based purely upon male symptoms.

infected with HIV. And, in the United States, someone develops AIDS every 17 seconds. The scourge of AIDS will not disappear in the foreseeable future, but research continues. If governments would increase funding for research into better treatment and an eventual cure of AIDS, people who are HIV positive or who have AIDS, as well as their partners, families and friends, would be more hopeful.

AIDS has raised many questions in our society. Because the people first infected were often marginalized by church and society, they suffered needless discrimination and pain. Often parents and families felt a certain shame when they found their son had AIDS. When friends would ask what was wrong with their son who had lost so much weight, often the answer was: "He has cancer." Thus, parents were caught in a vicious cycle which made it impossible for their son or themselves to receive much needed comfort and support from family and friends.

Social and religious factors have created a stigma around AIDS that must be removed. AIDS is a disease, not a sin. Various denominations have issued statements urging solidarity with those who are living with AIDS. This is fine, but it's hardly enough. What is required is a radical shift in beliefs, values and attitudes. If the churches do not adhere to the Gospel which refuses to judge and condemn, then their declarations of solidarity are nothing more than meaningless words to which no one will pay attention.

The lives and spirituality of people living — and dying — with AIDS profoundly challenge the Christian community. They challenge us to realize that we form one body, one community. We human beings are so one in Jesus Christ that we must say, "We have AIDS." Indeed, we are *all* suffering, hoping and living with AIDS. And we are challenged to rediscover the God of Love revealed in Jesus Christ as well as a lifestyle of authenticity which enables us to *feel* with all human beings in their joy and their pain.

What is spirituality?

A while ago I went to the hospital to visit a friend living with AIDS. Harry, who had been ill for several weeks, was hospitalized after his partner of several years had died. Harry had taken care of John faithfully even though he himself was not feeling well. They had been very happy together, despite the rough spots which enter into any relationship. Now Harry was alone. He was no longer John's partner. A young man in his thirties, Harry was facing a life which he hoped would be healthy and long, but which he knew deep down was going to be rather short and painful.

He had seen John deteriorate physically and mentally over the last year or so. And he had seen others tread the same path — too many others: young, vibrant, loving men and women whose future hopes and dreams had been smashed by this detestable Acquired Immune Deficiency Syndrome (AIDS). Harry knew that he was on this path as well, but, like the others, he still hoped it would somehow be different. He was determined to live. He and John had been very close and together for so long that now he said to me, "My task is to find out who Harry is. For a long time, I was known as 'John's partner.' Now that is over and I have to find 'Harry.'" He wondered whether he would ever find someone else with whom he could fully share his life, his love of the arts, his hopes and his fears. He wondered if he would ever again have someone with whom he could express his love sexually. There were so many unanswered questions. But now was not the time to answer these questions. He was too busy fighting off some unknown thing within his body that was causing him constant, uncontrollable diarrhea. He had to concentrate, to muster his energies to *live*.

The days dragged on. Things got worse. He was wasting away. This handsome young man looked much older than his years. Yet, his blue eyes remained bright, especially the one day I came in and he said, "I've just read a psalm which says it all for me — except for verses 19-22 which seem not to fit at all. Anyway, I love it. It is Psalm 139. Would you read it for me? But leave out those verses." I did and it was an experience I will never forget. As I read these words for Harry, *he* relaxed and brightened, and *I* felt as if I were hearing these words myself for the very first time: "O Lord, you have searched me and known me. You know when I sit down and when I rise up; you discern my thoughts from far away. You search out my path and my lying down, and are acquainted with all my ways. Even before a word is on my tongue, O Lord, you know it completely.... Such knowledge is too wonderful for me; it is so high that I cannot understand it.... For it was you who formed my inward parts; you knit me together in my mother's womb. I praise you, for I am fearfully and wonderfully made. Wonderful are your works; that I know very well..."

This marvellous moment of insight and faith, which I think Harry was more interested in having me experience personally than he was in relating his own experience to me, occurred amidst great pain and human suffering. The room still hung heavy with the smell of unrelenting diarrhea. The physical pain that wracked his body was quite evident. His embarrassment moved him to apologize. Yet, in this very dismal setting, Harry was aware of and meeting Someone else.

Despite the efforts of nurses and doctors, Harry's physical condition worsened daily. All that remained of his tall frame was a skeleton with loosely hanging skin. His eyes sunk deeper and deeper into his skull. My next visit found him sitting on the edge of his bed, finishing his breakfast: the first time he had even felt like eating for days. He was proud that he had got it down. When I came in, he greeted me rather happily and lay down on the bed. But he soon began to vomit violently for several minutes. Finally, the spasms finished and he lay back exhausted. Nevertheless, he looked at me and, with his eyes still bright and full of life, said: "It may not look like it, but God is *good!*"

In Harry's story we find a spirituality. This spirituality is not just the story of his sensing God's presence and goodness. His spirituality is his whole life: his life with John, his caring for him, his love of the arts, his sexuality, his relationships, his work, his body, his spirit, himself, his friends, his living with AIDS. His story reminds us that having a spirituality does not remove the pain and suffering, the anger, the bitterness, the despair, the horror of AIDS which can so utterly destroy a person. Herein lies the paradox of spirituality: while someone with AIDS lives and feels the pain and the losses involved, he or she also lives in, with and for a Transcendent which is taking on flesh in his or her very being. Spirituality is the lifestyle of a person relating to the Transcendent.

In Old Testament times, the Israelites thought of the human being as a whole. They did not divide the person into material parts and spiritual parts. Nor was the individual isolated from the community. One's lifestyle was deeply incarnational. In the history of their nation was revealed the God who was part and parcel of their lives. Through Moses and the prophets the Israelites discovered more and more deeply how their lives and their God were deeply entwined. Through Moses and the prophets, they dared to free themselves from slavery and move into the promised land. The covenant with the Lord encompassed their whole life. The Creator was with them, forming with them the People of God. They and their history were one. They were rooted, enfleshed. Their way of life with their God was forged out of this very rootedness in the earth with the Creator God, the Lord of History.

With Jesus Christ this same tradition of wholeness continued and deepened. Jesus came to make the people and the world whole. The salvation Jesus wrought was not just concerned with the spirits of individuals. It concerned the whole person and, indeed, the whole community to which the individual was joined by God's intimacy with humanity through Jesus Christ, the Word incarnate. Making Jesus and his teachings alive in each one and the whole group was the spirit which animated the community. The "spiritual" person was one who lived in the Spirit of God (I Corinthians 2:14-15). The accent is upon *lived*. Through their faith Christians came to live a bodily life, coloured by that Spirit of Jesus' own life. The same Spirit bound them together in a community. With time, however, this wholeness of the individual and the community was infected with dualism.

Over the centuries there slowly developed a suspicion of the body. Often the body was seen as something weighing down the person. Soon the ordinary believer began to think of a salvation limited to the soul. The body, with its desires, only kept people from the heavenly kingdom where their true home lay. Consequently, to have a spirituality and to be spiritual came more and more to mean directed towards the "other" world (heaven). "This" world in which mortal beings live and die was thought of as a place of exile, a valley of tears from which people needed to escape. In the process, there developed a whole practice of self-denial meant to get the body under control. The process accented the individual and one's determination to live in the world as if he or she were not in it. It was a process of trying to live like the bodiless spirits called angels. Set forms of prayer and the individualistic "imitation" of Christ were added to help the individual escape this world. Spirituality came to be seen as something in opposition to the body or matter. The scriptural sense of wholeness and of spirit as giving life lost its primacy and authentic Christian meaning on a practical level.

If we are to regain a proper sense of spirituality we must realize that spirituality is a unifying factor. It is much more than saying prayers and practising self-denial to escape this world. It is much more than trying to rid the soul of its bodiliness. Spirituality is much more inclusive.

Whole life

Spirituality, properly understood, is the whole life of a person lived in relationship with a transcendent value which calls out to us to abandon selfishness and self-centredness. Spirituality is simultaneously a call and a response. There is something outside me, yet very intimately related to me, that initiates a process of growth in this life. Beckoned by this transcendent value I engage my whole life in incarnating it. The call and the response are gifts that become flesh in my lifestyle, in all that I am living in the human community related to the Giver. But at the same time, our receiving is not simply a passive acceptance; rather, the receiving is an active yes, a commitment to living whatever is involved in the process of growth to which we are called. Our response is a breaking out of our self-obsession to realize that life is more than "me" and "my soul." There are realities, values, persons which are outside the whole self we are and which are in themselves gifts. By moving out of self and towards others we discover who we really are as persons living with others.

Relationship to others

We stand in relationship to others. We are not simply alone, the centre to which all must bow. Rather, in responding to this call, we see that we are who we are precisely by knowing, valuing, loving, supporting and being with others, and, indeed, the world itself. In short, the life process entails the totality of who we are as incarnated beings.

The "other" calls me to realize that my life is involved with the ongoing creation which is the progression of humanity. That which transcends me is that which calls me forward. I can refuse to respond. I can remain embedded in my life of selfishness. On the other hand, to say yes to this call is to commit myself to becoming the person I am called to be in relationship with others.

However, do not get me wrong. I am not talking about a call from some kind of "heavenly" thing. It is not a voice in an otherwise silent darkness. It is not a vision. It is a call which comes in and through creation, people, events, life itself. God has created us as body-soul persons. We are total beings of flesh and blood. Only through our incarnatedness do we hear and see the path which is the life we are living.

Years ago a friend of mine was just finishing his university studies and wondering what he would do for the rest of his life. He felt somehow that what he had learned should not be kept just to make a living for himself. It was the time of John F. Kennedy's presidency and he heard of the Peace Corps. "This is it," he thought. So he embarked on a life that led him to Africa where he taught science in an isolated village and where Africans taught him about what life really was. His experiences of Africa, his relationship with the African students, their families and with other Peace Corps members opened him up more and more to the real person he was. The rest of his life became a continuing response to life. He cherished life. He was determined to make his own life and the life of every person he encountered fuller. Indeed, making life and the human community more human and more loving became his avocation.

Each person has a background, culture and context. This is the stuff of which the call is made and in which the call to go beyond selfishness is heard and responded to. Everything we experience forms our life, and it is within this that we discover the key to becoming all that we are meant to be and thereby find fulfilment. Over a lifetime, the decisions we make, the people we meet, the events we live contain the stuff of our becoming the persons and the communities we are meant to be. The world of work, finances, politics, recreation, family and friends is our world. Here something will happen when the time is ripe. That event will challenge and call us to break out and to risk becoming the authentic persons we are meant to be.

True self

Every human being spends a lifetime creating an image — the person we want others to see. (And we often come to believe that this really is who we are.) The real "me," however, lies deep within. This authentic "me" is always there, but covered more or less heavily by our attempts to disguise it. Yet, with time, a partner, a friend, an event such as job loss or illness, or even someone's passing remark touches us. It hits home. One more part of the disguise crumbles. And this usually occurs in our interrelationships.

John of the Cross, a sixteenth-century Spanish mystic, told some nuns that they may have entered the monastery thinking that, since the sisters there wanted to be good and go to heaven, they would be really nice and kind, and life in the monastery would be great. Then he told them what they probably already knew from experience: this wasn't the case. The nun next to them was meant to be a problem for them! By that he meant that daily life with others will challenge us to see the rough parts of our very selves. Ordinary life with another human being is bound to make us see who we are because we cannot have everything our own way. Living with another, sharing life together, means letting go of certain things. We come to see in times of conflict or even in times of agreement that there are certain things in our personality and lifestyle of which we must let go *if* we want to become fully the person we are called to be in this life. Every conflict we experience, and all the previously hidden elements of the self we see because of it, are important parts of this life of ours. Everything in life is part of the process of spirituality.

Spirituality is a lifestyle — a life lived here and now in this bodily existence. It is a lifestyle centred upon a value, a transcendent reality to which we are called and a commitment to that which breaks us out of our self-imposed isolation and the false self we have so carefully constructed over a lifetime. This spirituality provides meaning to our lives.

Yet, is this Christian spirituality? The spirituality I have just described does not sit well with some — they would consider this a secular or non-religious approach to spirituality, certainly inferior to "Christian" spirituality. But I would argue that the spirituality described here is not a lesser or a lower path. This is the same path which all persons walk and live. However, if we speak of a spirituality which is Christian, it must have some specific characteristics. Let us see what they might be.

Christian spirituality

Since spirituality includes all aspects and dimensions of a person's life, the same is true for Christian spirituality. It is the life of a person committed to the God revealed in Jesus Christ and lived in the Spirit within the community. For a follower of Christ, a believer, spirituality is a life of incarnating the reality of Jesus by actively allowing the message of Jesus to shape his or her life. His is the message of love above all else: love of God and love of neighbour, both of which are inseparable (Mark 12:28-34). To love everyone without judgement is to love God.

Compassionate love

Our striving for transcendence, transformation and value is accomplished by love. Love breaks us out of our self-absorption and our obsession to possess things. This love, which Jesus manifested in his words and in his life, reveals itself by a deep compassionate relating to others.

Jesus' life is God's life here and now. Jesus enfleshed God's qualities in all that he was and did. Hence, as Christian believers, our spirituality is to incarnate that same living God through our mutual concern and ability to empathize. Empathy is not pity. Pity is not a Christian virtue: it is an attitude which suggests that we are better than the other. A Christian needs compassion — the ability to feel *with* the other. To be compassionate is to feel the other's joy and sorrow, the other's brokenness and wholeness, the other's dreams and reality. The compassionate person neither feels superior to nor looks down upon the other. When compassion prevails, a relationship of mutuality is established, and people relate as equals in life.

To repeat: our spirituality is a way of living. For a believer this means that love guides all that we do and are at work, in relationships, in our sexuality, and in our community. Love is the thread which runs through the whole of our very being. Love breaks us out of ourself and allows our authentic self to emerge and live. In being for others we discover and nourish the real persons we are.

Many persons living with AIDS have partners. They are committed to each other. Together they are partners in life sharing that life which is theirs in that developing love. There is a concern and a daring to feel with the other. Their own particularities sometimes create problems in the relationship, but their love binds them together in their joint attempt to find a path to a fruitful life. It means at times that this love and this concern will challenge each of them to let go and allow some aspect of their authentic self to come through. They express and reinforce their concern and love for each other in moments of intimacy. They relate as sexual beings. To relate sexually is not simply to have sexual intercourse. Relating sexually refers to the intimate experience of relating as human beings in an attitude of trust, openness and giving as well as receiving the other. It is not just genital activity. Sexuality is about human relating; it is an essential part of a couple's life and, therefore, an essential part of their Christian spirituality. Christian spirituality is not something invisible. It is of the spirit; it gives us life and breath as we live out that spirituality of commitment to God in our commitment to each other.

In community

We do this within a community of believers. No one is alone in this journey of life lived in God here and now. The person who believes contributes to the life of the community by the enfleshing of the love and compassion of God seen in Jesus. The community of believers in turn supports and nourishes the individual, for all are one. They form one body of Christ. Thus, what happens to one happens to all and vice versa.

A Christian spirituality is lived in *this time* and in *these circumstances*. This spirituality is an experience of the "concrete human being" within this concrete community. Believers living with AIDS experience life and God within the here and now, but in a way specific to themselves. For a spirituality cannot be constructed outside a person's experience of life; rather, we must begin with people's life experience and, in this case, as believers who are people living with AIDS.

In the following chapters I shall present what people living with AIDS have to say about their experience. Any further reflection will indeed be just that — a reflection upon what has been the experience and practice of those intimately involved in living with AIDS.

* * *

Further reading

Barlett, John G. and Ann K. Finkbeiner. *The Guide to Living with* HIV *Infection.* Baltimore and London: The Johns Hopkins University Press, 1992.

Fortunato, John E. AIDS: *The Spiritual Dilemma.* San Francisco: Harper & Row, 1987.

Hardy, Richard P. "Christian Spirituality Today." *Spiritual Life,* 28, 3 (1982): 151-160.

Schneiders, Sandra M. "Spirituality in the Academy." *Studies in Religion,* 62 (1990): 15-38.

2

Impasse
and
a loving God

Being diagnosed HIV positive or with AIDS starts the person down a whole new path of life — and the beginning of this journey is frightening. One's hopes and dreams seem to dissolve into nothingness. If someone is taking the HIV antibody test for the first time, the days or weeks before getting the results can be filled with anxiety. Time and time again, the person may go over the occasions on which the virus might have been contracted. One tries to remember each possibility and oftentimes thinks, "Well, there may be a possibility, but I really don't think I have it." Next day, the process begins again, but this time, perhaps, the person thinks differently: "Maybe, there was a chance. Maybe that person was infected and didn't know it." Or, in the case of others, "I feel fine and I was never promiscuous and I didn't share any needles. So, I am worrying for nothing." (Sometimes the person goes through this inner monologue even before deciding to take the test.) "What will I do if it turns out that I am positive?"

Some simply decide to wait and see. Others delve even more deeply into details of the past, present and future. Each person has his or her own way of deciding whether to be tested and of coping with the ordeal of waiting for the results.

When the results are ready and the person returns to the physician to find out, nervousness increases, and so does the anxiety level. In the waiting room, the person tries to convince himself or herself that everything will be fine: "This is it, but I really don't think it is possible. I've been safe."

Entering the physician's inner office, the person may try to determine the results by reading the doctor's face and body language. Sometimes, the doctor begins slowly explaining the meaning of the results, whether negative or positive. Sometimes the doctor, finding it so difficult to tell the person he or she is positive, simply blurts out: "I'm afraid I have bad news for you. The tests show that you are positive for the HIV antibodies." Others have been told even without the test: "You have what is called Pneumocystis Carinii Pneumonia and thrush. Therefore, you must have AIDS." Or, "Your blood tests for your skin condition show that your immune system is inordinately depressed. Only HIV could cause this. We'll take blood now for the HIV antibody test." (Fortunately, these latter statements from physicians are fewer and far between these days, but they are made. Remember, even doctors have difficulty facing the reality of this disease!)

Receiving the news that one is HIV positive or has AIDS means embarking on a new life path. Shock is usually the first reaction, and little of what the doctor says after those words of disclosure is heard. All one can think of is: "I'm going to die. What will I do?" The person may or may not ask questions about his or her condition: "How long do I have?" "Can there be some mistake?" "What can we do about it?" Some simply cry. Others try to deny it. Still others express their fears. Some are silent.

Over the days and weeks that follow, the HIV positive person has so much to think about. He or she often rides a roller coaster of denial, anger, hope, despair, fear, determination to live, and pugnacity. None of this seems fair or just. With whom will one share this burden? "If I tell my partner, will he (she) simply run away just when I need him (her) the most?" "What will my family think?" If the person is gay and has already told his family, he may wonder: "Is it worth causing my parents and sisters and brothers the pain and sadness?" If, on the other hand, the gay man has not come out to his family, he may wonder how to tell them both that he is gay and that he is HIV positive or has AIDS.

Telling others

When it comes to this disease, disclosure to others is fraught with the underlying homophobia so prevalent in our society. This irrational fear and hatred of gays and lesbians creates tremendous problems for the people living with AIDS. Every person, even the gay man who has come to terms with his gayness, has an internalized homophobia — at least to some extent. To acknowledge and accept oneself as good, and as loved by God as one is, is a lifelong task. Why? Because church and society have so often said that being gay is bad. Culture says being gay is abnormal, being heterosexual is not. Hence, homophobia is external as well as internal. To be gay is to be different, and culture says that, if you are different, you are not welcome. To have to deal with this attitude at so traumatic a time is gut-wrenching.

A number of factors make sharing this new element of life with others even more difficult. One must decide about health care, the treatments and drugs to take. "Who are the doctors best suited to join with me in facing and conquering this disease?" The person will wonder how long he can continue to work. Or he might wonder how he can afford the medical care, treatments and perhaps hospitalization. Then, there is the question of his own sexual expression. "Does this mean the end of my sexual life?"[1] "Did I get this disease from sexual intercourse? Did I pass on the virus? Will I be able to express my love in this way again?" A woman in her prime may resent the fact that possibilities of having children are torn out of her very being. These issues will surface and must be faced at some point.

Impasse

During this whole process, it often seems that, whatever way one turns, there is no solution. At times there is the overwhelming sense of being unable to control the situation. And for someone whose life has been built upon plans and control, this can be horrifying. The person seems caught in a situation of *impasse*. And when faced with this and all the unanswerable questions, the greatest temptation is simply to give up and say, "Why bother? It is hopeless and I will never get out of this anyway." Understandably some react with rage. They are caught and they are furious. With time many turn this rage to a constructive anger which enables them to live and, through their activism, to help others.

In the first years of the epidemic, a diagnosis indicating the presence of AIDS or the HIV was considered a death sentence. Our inability to treat HIV or AIDS meant people quickly developed diseases which greatly shortened their life. HIV and AIDS hung over all of them like an impenetrable dark cloud. Yet, even in the early days, some people lived for very long periods of time after being diagnosed with AIDS.[22] Today AIDS is spoken of as a "manageable chronic disease," but the spectre of

---

1. It is important to note that being diagnosed HIV positive or with AIDS does not mean the end of one's sexual expression of love.

2. For a superb book about long-time survivors, see Michael Callen, *Surviving* AIDS (New York: Harper-Collins, 1990).

death never goes away. The experience of powerlessness remains, especially right after diagnosis. Consequently, at the time one feels at the very least an ambivalence towards God. One may even give up on a God who would allow such a thing to happen. Yet, it is precisely within this very real experience of dead-end that one can find the potential for a fuller life here and now.

Sunset, midnight, dawn

Constance Fitzgerald, a Discalced Carmelite nun, speaks remarkably about impasse and its potential for growth and life.[33] Her article is based on St. John of the Cross'teaching about Christian growth and development. For John of the Cross, human life is a process, a journey to the full flowering of what it means to be authentically human here and now. This journey of life can be described as a movement from sunset through midnight to dawn. It begins when we take seriously human life with God now (sunset). We then face and pass through situations of impasse (dark night, midnight) before arriving at full life (dawn). Through this whole process, whether or not we are conscious of it at every moment, God remains with us. This is God's gift. Whatever the moment, whether of joy or sorrow, the immanent God stays, lives with and loves us.

While we believe that God is with us from the very beginning, our conscious entry into that process of life begins only when we take God seriously. It is a time of insight into what and who God is for us. Such an insight comes from God (gift) with the very events of our life. This insight may result from experiencing another's love for us or from discovering that personhood develops and grows in a love relationship with this

---

3. Constance Fitzgerald, "Impasse and Dark Night." In *Woman's Spirituality: Resources for Christian Development.* Edited by Joann Wolski Conn. (New York: Paulist Press, 1986), especially pp. 288 and 297.

person. Or, we may become aware that we are persons loved by God as we are; such an awareness often happens when some other human being's concern and love affirm our goodness. Or some event might lead us to realize that we are meant to live more authentically and that God is very much part of our lives. This is called conversion. Conversion is a radical decision to live out the best of who we see ourselves to be in relation to a God who has never abandoned us and who will never leave us orphaned.

A positive response to the call to live fully enables us to enter into a beautiful, indeed a marvellous, time. Life seems to take on full meaning. One wonders why one did not see it before. God seems so close and so utterly real to us that nothing could ever break that bond. This is the time of sunset.

Relate this to your own experience of *participating in,* not just observing, a beautiful sunset on a mountain peak or by the ocean. The colours and sounds are lively and life-giving. The hues of red, yellow and ochre and the varying shades of the blue sky with puffs of white clouds provide us with a "symphony of silent music" as John of the Cross would say. These colours join with the sound of the rustling of leaves on the mountain, the chirping of birds in the trees or the lapping of waves on the shore. This is an experience of transcendence here and now. Nothing could be greater and one wants to remain here, bathing in this beauty forever. In these beautiful experiences of human life and sensuality, we find our connection with God developing. We are literally bonding with the God of love. Sunset, however, is but a stage in the process.

Sunset is when we seriously begin trying to transcend ourself in order to discover our true self in full communion with God, others and all of creation. This time does not last forever. Little by little through days, weeks, months or years even, we are called and challenged to move deeper into the experience of God. Life challenges us to let go of our images of God, life and being. We have spent a lifetime creating a self which we project to others. *We* create a self which we want others to see and to know. Yet, deep within lies the authentic self which is being challenged to come forth for all to see. For this self to emerge, we must let go of all that is covering it. We must risk being authentic.

As we listen and respond to this challenge which reaches us in this life through people and events, there are times of hesitancy, even times of darkness. Gradually, our enthusiasm for communicating with God vanishes. God seems so distant now. We question why we should even bother with this God. These are times of night. The sun has set. Fading light surrounds us. What had seemed joyous and beautiful is now frightening and uncertain. We want to flee the approaching night for the security of light and comfort. We want to go home. We want to forget all we've heard about movement from beautiful light through darkness to the marvels of dawn. Why bother? Yet, we hang on, buffeted more and more by events which seem to tear us away from this time of calm and beauty which held so much hope and pleasure for us.

Then we arrive at the darkest part of the night — midnight. We have lost sight of everything which used to provide us with meaning and joy. Darkness surrounds us and fills us with anxiety. Fear of the unknown forms part of the risk-taking which our quest for authenticity demands of us. Here even God disappears. We sense we are dreadfully alone in hostile surroundings. All is dark and apparently hopeless.

In this obscurity hope seems foolish. Since there is no longer any meaning to this journey, we question the existence of God. "Some say that pain, loss or suffering is God's punishment. Well, I don't need a God like that." What we thought was God seems but the figment of our imagination. We might say, "Forget all this nonsense. Life is here and now. It is what I can feel and see. Death is simply a big dark void. There is nothing more!" John of the Cross poignantly describes this part of the journey as the dark night of the spirit: "At this stage persons suffer from sharp trials in the intellect, severe dryness and distress in the will, and from the burdensome knowledge of their own miseries in the memory, for their spiritual eye gives them a very clear picture of themselves. In the substance of the soul they suffer abandonment, supreme poverty, dryness, cold and sometimes heat. They find relief in nothing, nor does any thought console them, nor can they even raise the heart to God, so oppressed are they by this flame. This purgation resembles what Job said God did to him: You have changed to being cruel toward me [Job 30:21]. For when the soul suffers all these things jointly, it truly seems that God has become displeased with it and cruel. . . . A person's sufferings at this time cannot be exaggerated."[4]

Here we find an incredibly accurate description of what people living with AIDS go through during and even after diagnosis. The fear, the confusion, the anxiety, the anger, the absence of God, the physical and psychological suffering — all are part of the "dark night." Yet the dark night can also be a growth-producing experience, a possibility for an integration and transcending transformation into full human life.

Impasse implies that there is no way out. There seems to be no rational solution to the concrete problems people are facing. John of the Cross maintains that impasse and the experience of it contain the potential for transformation and the discovery of the authentic, whole self. However, that potential can be actualized only by entering into the experience rather than giving up and running away from it. The experience must become "my own." This happens when one yields, or surrenders, to it. There is no other way a person can unlock the potential of impasse.

Nonetheless, this surrender is not fatalistic. It is not a matter of saying: "Well, that's it. There is nothing I can do. I might

---

4. John of the Cross, *The Living Flame of Love.* In *The Collected Works of St. John of the Cross.* Translated by Kieran Kavanaugh and Otilio Rodriguez. (Washington: ICS Publications, 1991), pp. 648-649.

as well give up. It's hopeless." This would be a passive surrender in which we allow the impasse to control and direct us. An impasse can transform us only when our yielding is an active surrender with all the risk which that entails. This surrender says "Yes!" to God. This is an affirmation of hope, which dares to live out whatever the experience contains for the person in the present moment. Yet, this yes implies a determination to *live* out whatever it will hold in the future. It is a "Yes" to a God who loves and who desires wholeness and authenticity for the person. That "Yes" means that the person dares to seek out all available means to *live* fully this particular moment of life and all the moments which follow. It is a decision to *live*, not just to subsist, with AIDS.

The suffering and new experience of existence which aids brings are elements contributing to the transforming movement towards full life and authenticity. However, something more is needed. By daring to accept and to live the situation, the person finds the transforming potential in its horror.[5] The individual must enter the experience of darkness with all the feelings of anger, fear, frustration, wanting it not to be — and dare to say to oneself and indeed to God that one can find the transforming part of it. In the brokenness, powerlessness and poverty of the experience, the person can reach and be reached by the loving God in this dark mystery.[6]

How is this possible? How can someone discover a God of love in this ugly situation? Some have done it by fighting with God and venting their rage towards God and the world until they were exhausted. As they did, an answer began to glimmer

5. See Robert Isles, *The Gospel Imperative in the Midst of* AIDS: *Towards a Prophetic Theology* (Wilton, CT: Morehouse Publishing, 1989), p. 181, where he speaks of the new identity discovered in the surrender becoming a transforming experience. According to Albert J. Ogle, "Transformation: Visions and Plans," in *ibid,* p. 205, the challenge is to somehow find God's love and activity within the tragic experience of being alive with AIDS.

6. See Constance Fitzgerald, "Impasse and Dark Night." In *Woman's Spirituality: Resources for Christian Development,* pp. 297-298.

faintly in their consciousness. Over a period of weeks and months, they eventually came to an accommodation which led to a commitment to *live* life in an increasingly constructive way. Some tried, instead, to see the beauty around them: the love of their partner, friends and family; the wonder of spring flowers breaking through the thin layer of snow; the sparkling sun on the waters of the river just beyond their bedroom window. Still others found God by helping others go through this horrible situation by creating love and beauty for them. Others experienced God's presence by their activism in AIDS education, sharing their experience with others in groups or individually. In all this, as the disease progressed, new elements entered the picture and caused changes. A serene expectation awaits its fulfilment until the reality behind Harry's words became theirs: "It may not look like it, but God is good."

The God of love

Many people with AIDS have felt deep pain at the relentless condemnation of those "Christians" who shout out that God is punishing them for their evil lives. Those who are gay or who have used intravenous drugs are all too familiar with the God of hate which some Christians preach. At the "AIDS and Theology" conference held in Toronto, Ontario, in September 1991, one man told us how he had given up on this spiteful deity that had been preached to him from as far back as he could remember. This god was constantly trying to catch him doing something wrong so that he could either punish him right then and there or get him after he died. This loathsome god, so often spoken of and even preached about from some pulpits, is not the God of Jesus. A divine fear monger is hardly the One with whom we can build a healthy relationship!

Others have described similar experiences. Ron mentioned that after growing up in the Catholic church and hearing almost exclusively about this god of punishment, he finally decided: "I have better friends than this kind of god. I don't need him." This "kind of god" can make people judgemental of gays and lesbians. As one person said: "When we are well, people say we are queers, degenerates who should die and go to hell. But when we are sick, they want to 'minister' to us. Frankly, we do not want that shit!"

Most gay people reject this god which has been presented to them as the Christian God. In so doing, they are not rejecting God. Rather they are rejecting the false god which fundamentalists in all religions have created in their own image. Julian Filochowski, who is the chair of the Caritas Internationalis Working Group on AIDS, says it well: "Those who pretend that AIDS is God's punishment on a sinful section of our society have a vengeful God, a clumsy God and certainly not our Christian God of forgiveness, life and love."[7] Fortunately, many gays and lesbians believe in the God made known in Jesus Christ, the God who is completely different from the law enforcement deity some would have us believe in. This God is a God of love, of concern. This God even dares to be with all human beings and to suffer with us. This is the God of whom many people with AIDS speak — a God of love, of compassion, of life,[8] of forgiveness, of concern. With this God of Jesus, there are no throwaways. There are no rejects. Every single human being is of infinite value in the eyes of this God.[9]

God wants love to fill the whole of creation. Throughout the Scriptures, we find a God whose proclamation is the law of love — to love God and neighbour. When a scribe asked Jesus which was the greatest commandment, Jesus responded quite clearly, saying, "The first is, 'Hear O Israel: the Lord our God, the Lord is one; you shall love the Lord your God with all your heart, and with all your soul, and with all your mind, and with

7. Julian Filochowski, "A Measure of Our Humanity." *Catholic International*, 2, 20 (1991):963.

8. See Michael Callen, *Surviving AIDS*, p. 84

9. See Letty Russell (ed.), *The Church with AIDS: Renewal in the Midst of Crisis*. Louisville: Westminster/John Knox, 1990, pp. 39, 40-41, 62.

all your strength.'The second is this, 'You shall love your neighbour as yourself.'There is no other commandment greater that these" (Mark 12:28-31). These are Jesus'two basic commands.

Those who follow Jesus are those who love each other as Jesus himself loved people (John 13:34). Harmony is meant to be the atmosphere of human life, not confict, condemnation, death, hatred or retribution. In fact, in writing to his community, John underscores the necessity of authentic love as he writes, "For this is the message you have heard from the beginning, that we should love one another. We must not be like Cain who was from the evil one and murdered his brother. . . . We know that we have passed from death to life because we love one another. Whoever does not love abides in death. All who hate a brother or sister are murderers, and you know that murderers do not have eternal life abiding in them. We know love by this, that he laid down his life for us — and we ought to lay down our lives for one another. How does God's love abide in anyone who has the world's goods and sees a brother or sister in need and yet refuses help?" (I John 3:11-12, 14-17). Every human being is our sister and brother. Jesus'command means that all are worthy of the ultimate gift of love — one's own life. In Jesus, we find the incarnation of who God is. Jesus went to the limit to show that only love enables us to live a fully human life.

Of course we do find many references to God as judge in the New Testament. However, God's judgement seeks out the positive and the negative: God affirms those who have loved in their own way according to their capacity. God looks upon them loving and bringing harmony into the human community and says: "It is good." Negatively, God is concerned with the lack of love — a lack which destroys harmony and causes human beings to live in fear and as objects of hatred. However, above all God lives where there is love. In love, God is with the lovers and the lovers are with God. St. John of the Cross summed it up when he noted that all will be judged only on how much they have loved.

Persons living with AIDS are not long in discovering and placing their trust in this God who lives in love, despite the condemnations of some "religious" people. They dare to see, affirm and live in the God revealed in Jesus. In this relationship with the God of love, people find the truth of the Gospel — the truth which makes them free to live fully (John 8:31-32). Blessed by God with this living truth in their lives, fear, discrimination and hatred no longer control their lives. Thus, they are enabled to *live* with AIDS, not simply die. Despite the pain and the suffering, their gospel view of God as love allows them to trust this God to be with them. So blessed, they come to appreciate every element of creation and life, and that all are the beloved of God.

God loves all, especially the weakest and most oppressed by society. And God suffers with all! No one is alone in their pain and rejection. The God of Jesus is not an apathetic God, incapable of suffering. The cross of Jesus is this God's symbol of commitment to each and every person — a commitment which says, "I am with you always. I suffer with you. I rejoice with you."[10] This bespeaks an intimacy between God and humanity. Yet, it is not just the passion, suffering and death of Jesus which speaks of this closeness. It is the whole story of Jesus — his life, death and resurrection. In him, we discover the living God who indeed lives with us, taking part in the struggles, the vissicitudes and joys of life. At times we feel that presence with us. At other times we do not. Yet, whatever the feeling, there is the conviction — sometimes with a question — that somehow our God is with us.

Sometimes to affirm this presence of God in love is very difficult. As a person living with AIDS, one is faced with the fact

---

10. See William A. Doubleday, "Sin and Sickness/Faith and Health." In *The Gospel Imperative in the Midst of* AIDS: *Towards a Prophetic Theology,* p. 133.

that one's life may be shortened substantially. This means that the time one had counted upon to accomplish certain things — family, relationships, career — is so reduced that dreams may fade. And then the question "Why? Why me?" comes to the fore. Rejection by a fearful family, friend or partner must often be endured along with the physical pain of the disease. Yet, while these negative experiences are all too real, one must never forget that one is not alone — despite what one may feel at times.

The sense of impasse may come back time and again, here and there. It may seem to an individual that God has rejected him or that he has rejected God. Whatever the feeling, whatever the time, the person must dare to believe, to remember that God is with him or her in a loving, caring way. One day when I was visiting Ron, just weeks before he died, he said to me: "The old tapes keep playing back and all I can do in the face of this fear that God is hateful and punishing is to affirm what I believe: God loves me compassionately and fully." Those who come to know the God of Jesus realize that God is so clearly all that they have ever desired that they cannot really reject God; furthermore, they know that from the very beginning God has so loved the world that God cannot reject it or anyone in it without rejecting himself. In the face of this, they can only reject the god of hate and punishment.

Hence, the first element of a spirituality of a person living with AIDS is the affirmation and reception of the loving God made known to us in Jesus Christ. To affirm this God also means to accept all that one is personally. Self-acceptance means seeing the whole of who one is and has been and saying, "Yes, all this is me, and it's this me God loves with an infinite love." Gradually, the knowledge that God accepts me totally, and loves me as I am, grows in intensity. I realize more and more that God loves *me* as I am with all that I am, not despite who I am.

This is perhaps one of the most difficult things to internalize. For, so often, people hear that God hates them and judges them as sinners. People may affirm that God will forgive them, but the accent is always on the negative element. But, mutual acceptance between God and the individual means a transformation process begins in the particular circumstances of the person's life. The transformation engages the person on the continuing journey towards the fullness of life, in a deepening, active love for self and others. The transformation then involves an intimacy with this God of unconditional love who moves the person with AIDS to a deeper level of interpersonal communication.

* * *

Further reading

Callen, Michael. *Surviving* AIDS. New York: Harper-Collins Publishers, 1990.

Fortunato, John. AIDS: *The Spiritual Dilemma.* San Francisco: Harper & Row, 1987.

Iles, Robert H. (ed). *The Gospel Imperative in the Midst of AIDS. Towards A Prophetic Pastoral Theology.* Wilton, CT: Morehouse Publishing, 1989.

McNeil, John J. *Taking A Chance on God: Liberating Theology for Gays, Lesbians, and Their Lovers, Families and Friends.* Boston, MA: Beacon Press, 1988.

3

Aware
of God,
aware of life

As they grow in intimacy and knowledge of the God of love and compassion, people living with AIDS enter into a process of communicating — of prayer. Ron said of prayer: "Through prayer, and in the Holy Spirit, arrogance can be dissolved and love regained. Repentance and conversion — re-alignment and rebirth — are the only cures for the arrogant heart." For him, prayer was both the means of making contact with God and the means of harmonizing his love and life. In prayer, which is an awareness of God's presence with us, we come to see who we really are and to know God's presence in our life and love. When we realize that God loves us, we can begin to leave arrogance and the false self behind and truly affirm the authentic self. Prayer becomes a means of moving into authenticity and the hope of continued growth in this life in the world. The conversion of which Ron speaks is not "rebirth" in the sense of starting anew, while dismissing all that has gone before. The "rebirth" is a new awareness that one's entire life (including the past, which is now seen as an integral part) is a very necessary part of the whole journey. Prayer is the means of making this happen.

Speaking with God

Prayer can and does take many forms. Prayer can include verbally expressing one's needs, hopes, desires, dreams, anger, and love, not only to the self but to God. Prayer is the consciousness that this God of love actually loves me. This love allows me to tell God everything without fear. Divine love is constant, and I know that God will respond positively to me. I can be angry and express that anger to God. Just as a couple who have lived happily together for fifty years know that the anger that explodes in the partner occasionally is not really directed against him or her but is an expression of fear or frustration, so God undertands human anger and does not respond with fire and brimstone. God loves and sees deep within, knowing the sources of our feelings (Psalm 139).

This prayer allows me to see who I really am — with all my good, and not-so-good, points. As I speak with the God who is present, I develop that sense of freedom to be who I really am with God. In so doing I come to an awareness of what is important in life. I can see my priorities — what they have been and what they might be. Until I dare to speak my mind, as it were, I remain at the surface. The masks that we wear in life — the masks we have created — become what we think we are. But prayer as speaking reveals who we are to ourselves and to God; verbally expressing our needs, wants and feelings allows us to see what lies beneath. Often this is the person we have been trying to be all our lives, but never dared to be for fear that friends or intimate companions along life's journey would reject us. Thus, in and through prayer, we learn where we can grow, what we need to receive and what we need to let go of in life.

But you don't need a denominational identity to pray. You don't have to belong to a particular church. There are many people with AIDS whose faith transcends organized religion. But this fact does not remove them from the loving presence of God. While some persons living with AIDS have felt it necessary to drop their affiliation with their churches because of past experiences, others remain, choosing those elements important to their continued growth. Still others feel that their church left *them,* but they continue to believe in God.

One man living with AIDS liked to pray in an empty church building. There was something about the quietness, the darkness or perhaps the simplicity of it which allowed him to commune more intimately with God. He found that an empty church stirred up positive memories which had given him life and hope as a child or young man. That same sense of connectedness came through. Now, he felt with God, as it were. He had given up the church because of the crushing oppression and rejection he had experienced as a gay man, and now as a gay man with AIDS. Yet, this did not prohibit him from using the "sacramental reality" and atmosphere of the church building to be and to commune with God.

Another man found he could be consciously with God by walking along the seashore. The power of the ocean — sometimes with its gentle lapping waves, sometimes with rough, turbulent crashing torrents of water — offered him a certain resonance with his various moods at different times. It was expansive too. On the seashore he was alone with the Transcendent. This ocean experience was a means of becoming conscious of God's presence in a tangible way — a sacrament. The sound of the waves, the sight of the blue-green expanse, the feel of the sand and water on his bare feet — these made him open to God's presence and allowed him to speak with this Creator who is in all things and deep within the very person that he was.

One friend of mine loved to get out into the quiet of nature, particularly by hiking up a mountainside. The exertion expended to reach the peak reminded him of the energy required and used to live life fully. There were times when he felt too exhausted to continue the hike. But a short rest to catch his breath gave him new power. His times with God were like this, he thought. The roughness of the rocks beneath his feet kept him conscious of his rootedness in the earth. The sometimes uncertain gravelly path reminded him of his childhood when he used to play on the little hillside near his home. Even as a youngster he felt that someone greater, someone loving was with him. He delighted in finally arriving at the peak and looking at the countryside's beauty. All these thoughts, and the words if there were any, were prayer — a consciousness of the Transcendent. Each person talks to God in his or her own way.

As one speaks with God one sometimes asks for help or healing or remembering or reconciling. Some call this prayer of petition, or intercessory prayer. And this is good. There are times when an individual with AIDS seeks things from God. The person may want to be healed from this illness which is so physically and psychologically draining. It may be that the person wants to trust and be open to someone who is loved, yet cannot find the courage. So, one may ask for that as well. Praying in this way helps a person admit that there is a power greater than oneself. At the same time, this helps a person see what he or she needs to do and can do. St. Augustine said that if we pray thinking we are going to change God's mind, we are wrong. Prayer is not meant, he said, for that; rather, prayer teaches us what we need and what we can do to meet that need. Petitionary prayer means asking God for something. When we pray this way we simply verbalize our felt needs at that time. Verbalization makes us more than ever aware of our need of the Other. Quite often this type of prayer helps us see how we can help ourselves. Yet, there is a mystery about this prayer; for somehow, through it, God seems to give us what we cannot attain by ourselves.

As long as we live, we shall continue to seek things and hope from God. Often this seeking becomes more an effort to be open to all that life offers us than a quest to get things. We seek to be with God in love, and to affirm our readiness to experience all that life contains. Ultimately we are talking about a sense of prayer as communion, as oneness, with God.

To be with God when one has the energy to do so: this is prayer. There are times when there is no energy to put into praying. One is simply too tired or completely unable to concentrate; the illness is too overwhelming. Yet, while one cannot pray as before, that experience has established a relationship with God. Ironically, though there may be only a fleeting thought or awareness of God, this can be perhaps the deepest prayer of one's life. Petitionary prayer becomes the binding cord of life between the person, the community, God and the whole of creation with all its remarkable beauty. In and through prayer the world takes on a new brilliance and beauty. One sees the world in a new light, even if one is not conscious of the seeing, but only of the pain or darkness.

Not surprisingly, when one lives with AIDS, one prays. The need to be in contact with that which forms the life and spirit of all is strong. One wants to know and feel all that one can. And what better way than to be consciously in union with the Creator and Sustainer of all life?

Meditation

Another way of communing with God is called meditation. In various religious traditions, meditation has always been very important. Each tradition has its own ways of entering into a mental relationship with the source of life. Each uses its own symbols. Each has its own imagery. It might be a mantra, a chant, a tonka, mandala or prayer beads. All are tools of communion with God.

Visualization is also a tool, or technique, and it is quite popular among people living with AIDS. Taking time to be with God or life or nature through visualization is a form of meditative prayer. While it has been around for a long while, the idea of visualization has come into its own during this past decade or so with the advent of AIDS.

Visualizations are various forms of therapy based upon the idea that the mind can have a real effect upon the total person — not just one's intellectual, but one's bodily dimension, too. Using this technique, a therapist might encourage the individual to imagine (visualize) love flowing into, within and over the whole body. The person forms a mental image of love as a wave flowing over, gently washing and healing him or her. Then, that same loving flow becomes a waterfall gently cascading through the head, flowing through every crevice of the person's body, healing the person's every wound.

For others the visualization takes on a more active, almost combative imagery. They might imagine healthy cells destroying each cell infected with HIV in a simple, almost effortless, way. The body clears itself of infection throughout the visualization. Others visualize calm and peaceful scenes of natural beauty and harmony. This enables them to reduce stress and restore the harmony of the elements of the body.

Often breathing exercises go hand in hand with the visualizations. For example, you can seat yourself comfortably in a quiet, serene atmosphere. Then, you form a mental image of God or some person as a quiet, gentle light or even as a spirit in the distance. But this light, person or spirit is visualized as being at your very core, in your very heart. You breathe in all that surrounds you (all the beautiful things around you, the joys and loves, as well as all the thoughts, fears, distresses and pains tossing about in your mind). All these flow into the light or the person imagined. The light then becomes more brilliant, the person glows, the spirit brightens. This means that all these things are being transformed, purified, made into love. Then, these things are exhaled into the world through the heart and completely changed into love. By repeatedly combining breathing and imaging, this exercise produces peace and calm within the person. Stress disappears. Some prefer to use Christian images which speak of the love, peace and hope they want to receive. These techniques of breathing and imaging reduce stress and heal in a variety of ways. When used in the context of Christian faith, they become Christian meditative forms.

Many people meditate using scriptures. Some rely on nature. The point is to use whatever helps the mind relate to the Transcendent peacefully and with serenity. Ignatius of Loyola recommends a process similar to what follows. From the scriptures (the Bible) you read a gospel passage about Jesus, for example. Then, put yourself in the story and, in your imagination, take part in that event in Jesus' life. Having done that, you gradually move into a reflection on what this means for you in your life. Finally, you decide to do something that day to make the world a more human place for all. Or, you may simply reflect on the meaning of certain phrases or passages from the Bible, rather than use imagery. In all these meditations, the accent is upon the activity of the individual's imagination and thought process.

There are other forms of meditation, of course. John Main, a Benedictine monk, offered us an approach which is a path of silence. Drawing from the whole Christian tradition, Main saw meditation as "remaining still at the centre." He said, "In meditation we simply stand before God, we open ourselves to his presence, we wait upon the Lord." [1] His particular practice of meditation stands midway between the imaginative type of meditation we spoke of earlier and contemplation. Main suggested that the person find a special word or phrase (what

---

1. See Paul Harris, "An Explanation of Christian Meditation." *Catholic New Times,* 21 March 1993 (Vol. 17, No. 6, p. 4).

Eastern religions call a "mantra") and repeat that word "love" or "peace" or "gentleness" or whatever. For twenty or thirty minutes one sits comfortably in a quiet place conducive to drawing inward and repeats that word or phrase.

This activity opens one up to the reality of God. It produces a stillness in the deepest centre of our being. That word or phrase falls gently and graciously into one's very centre and remains there giving life, peace, hope, serenity. That which is called upon is produced within. The Transcendent takes hold and, as it were, awakens within us. God has always been there, but now God seems to awaken. Actually, it is we who are awakening to God, as John of the Cross reminds us.

Another meditative approach is the rosary or beads. This is something with which most Catholics are familiar. Unfortunately, over the past century, its original value and purpose has been tainted by misuse and ideological purposes. Originally, the beads, which are very similar to the Buddhist and Islamic beads, were meant as tactile aids to establish a connection with the Transcendent. The handling of the beads led to a meditative silence in which the person opened up to God, to Light. The physical sensation of the movement of the beads through the fingers (fingering the beads), the constant repetition of the same words for each bead, the directive to think about a particular event in the life of Christ or simply to be open to God — all produce a sense of personal relation with our immanent God.

The activity also produces physical changes in the praying person. The person relaxes. Worries, troubles, fears take second place now. There is an immense physical peace and calmness which enters into the individual or, rather, flows from the centre of his or her being. This peace lasts even after the prayer is finished, for a while at least. By helping the person to relax, the prayer of the beads allows us to leave things aside and enter into a particular and conscious relationship with God. A person living with AIDS might find this prayerful, meditative exercise useful: it can and does reduce stress and combines the physical and spiritual elements beautifully, thereby encouraging human wholeness and personal integration.

One can meditate using music, the beauty of which can open us again to God. Gregorian chant is particularly useful and is similar to the beads in terms of its meditative and physical qualities. Anyone who chants discovers that the breathing techniques required to chant provide a bodily rhythm leading to relaxation and stress reduction. The listener may also have the same experience, at least to some degree. So, sitting in a particular, homey, comfortable setting and listening to the chant, one will find oneself opening up to God — sometimes just being there with God, sometimes actually speaking with God, sometimes thinking about God in Jesus perhaps.

Whatever symbols, techniques or particular practices a person living with AIDS uses, a meditative prayerfulness is beneficial for both spirit and body. Done in a peaceful, relaxed manner, adapted by and to the person who prays, meditation fosters personal contact with self, others and God. God's presence is more keenly felt. And this, after all, is the object of prayer.

Many people living with AIDS speak of being spiritual but not religious, meaning that they believe in God, but do not belong to any particular denomination. They pray. They relate life to God and God to life. They have a deep sense of God's abiding presence and love for them and their love for God. Prayer for them is a way of becoming close to God, a way of spending time with God who is their friend.

For many people with AIDS, especially gay persons, their denominations are little more than institutions of condemnation, judgement and oppression. Many left, rejecting the god their denominations preached. Yet, they have never really rejected God. Their various experiences in life have led some to see that God in Christ never rejected or condemned them. When they rediscover this God of life and love, they see how institutional Christianity has often hindered God's coming to them rather than opened the way for them to God. So, they develop their spiritual dimension apart from the religious practices of organized religion.

A diagnosis of HIV or AIDS puts people on the edge, perhaps at the point of impasse. Often, the spirituality which has always been there — perhaps without their having realized it — comes to the fore. For some this is a difficult process because of the hatred and oppression they experienced in their former churches. They find it difficult to separate faith in God — which they most definitely have — from some church. For others, the separation is much easier. In any case, if they can leave aside the institutional deformations and open themselves to the God who loves them, they find a strength and a peace to live with AIDS. Some find that peace by a return to the church they had left. Some find that peace by a partial connection with that institution. This reconnection is valid and good if it helps them to find the God of peace and love. Most, however, find their path in spirituality, not in the moral precepts of organized religion.

Contemplation

Prayer is consciousness of God, and it is customarily expressed in words, petitions or imagining. There is, however, another form of prayer which opens us even more to God, to others and to the world. While most types of prayer involve activity, contemplation is more an attitude — an attitude of openness and receptivity. John of the Cross tells us that contemplation is to receive. To be able to receive God — this is pure gift. In receiving God, we receive the whole of reality because God is never separate from reality. This is the beauty of contemplation. In contemplation God enables us to listen, to be open to all.

Nothing we can do can make contemplation exist within us. In the more popular view of contemplation, it is something we do. We sit and concentrate our whole being, heart and soul, on God or an object. It is our activity. But in the Christian tradition, contemplation is God's activity in us. God gives contemplation as gift and we receive it. It is part of the mutuality process established between God and us. Other forms of prayer are a preparation for contemplation which may or may not be given. Prayer opens us to the possibility. In contemplation God activates that potential when God wants.

Contemplation is that prayer in which God enables us to let go of the ways we use to determine the place each thing or person holds in our lives. It means accepting what is as it is without demanding that it be different and classified the way we want things to be. Contemplation is a deconstruction of our egocentric way of seeing so that reality can appear to us as it really is.

This can happen precisely because the person is becoming more and more intensely one with God, more and more one with all that is. Since God is one with all of creation, as we become one with God, we become one with everything as well.

Without necessarily speaking of God, many people living with AIDS speak of seeing things as if for the very first time. Having experienced impasse, having been on the margins, all things take on a newness which is wonderful. Ron used to speak to me of how wonderful the spring flowers were. He seemed more than usually delighted to see the rabbit which roamed his backyard. He was enthralled with the beauty of the garden and trees. Others have described experiencing the same kind of openness and newness and delight in seeing things in this powerful way.

Time and time again, persons living with AIDS comment on how they are seeing the world with new eyes. They are living the present moment and seeing things that before might have slipped by unnoticed. This is all part of the process of contemplation; it is something which is given or it is not had at all.

Contemplation is an attitude of openness and availability to the whole of creation. Discovering God, persons living with AIDS discover life and all that makes it up. They really desire to sense it all. Yet, the struggle to live with AIDS forces people to realize and feel intensely the pain and anguish of not being in control even as they sense the wonder of the reality which surrounds and fills them. Everything is lived to the full. They do not experience its intensity all the time. It comes and goes. There are times when they wonder if it ever was there at all — so great is the physical pain or the sense of isolation or abandonment. Waves of joy and rocks of despair remain part of the experience of life. Yet, contemplation helps provide a foundation , a hope, a strength to dare to risk all and go on with this God whom we know is with us.

Contemplation makes one more sensitive to life and all that constitutes it. It enables us to see people and love them. It enables us to experience peace and pain, anguish and hope more intensely. In real life pain, darkness and death co-exist with beauty, wonder and creativity. But one must experience this dialectic to be truly aware of its reality in human life.

There is an intensity of bodiliness in the contemplative sense of openness to God. It is sensuality experienced at its depth. One is aware most deeply of how marvellous and important it is to *feel*, indeed to be body. To be separated from that bodiliness is excruciating. When John of the Cross lay dying of an extremely painful disease which covered his legs and back with deep and ugly ulcers, he received holy communion. Immediately afterwards a monk noticed that he was crying and, thinking it might be because he was in much pain, asked him, "Why are you crying?" John paused and answered with deep sadness in his voice, "Because this will be the last time that I will see my Lord in this way." There was a letting go of bodiliness, of sacramentality, of being enfleshed which was extremely painful for him. He would not allow the idea of eternal life to remove that pain. He faced this dilemma in all its devastating reality: he knew how much it meant.

I had a very dear friend who was dying from complications due to AIDS. He lived in another city. I called him one day, and, during our conversation, he began to cry, saying between bursts of heartfelt tears, "I won't ever see you again." He and I had talked at some length a week before when I was with him. He knew that after death we would be still close, though in a very different way. Yet he, like I, wept at the change. For we are human beings with bodies, and our ways of relating and being are simultaneously bodily and spiritual. Take one of those elements away and we are crushed.

Contemplation enables us to find ways of being intensely in life, in bodiliness and moving towards wholeness. Persons living with AIDS, when gifted with contemplation, find others and God in a new depth. There is great love. There is greater desire. There is greater passion. There is greater compassion. Anger remains and may flare up, but it does so in a constructive way. The focus of life is now the other: people, nature and God.

* * *

Further reading

Hardy, Richard P. *Streams in the Wasteland.* Pasay City, Philippines: Saint Paul Publications, 1984.

Johnston, William. *Christian Zen.* San Francisco: Harper & Row, 1971.

Tilleraas, Perry. *The Color of Light: Meditations for All of Us Living with* AIDS. San Francisco: Harper & Row, 1988.

4

Love — fullness of life

He was really tired. He had lost count of the days since his last full night's sleep. Some days he longed for those hours of solid sleep where nothing disturbed him. But it had been so long ago, he wondered if he would ever have a sleep like that again. His partner of ten years had been home after a severe bout with PCP. A month had passed. He did not seem to be recovering all that well. He seemed to be getting weaker and weaker, though the PCP was under control. Steadily, another virus was gnawing away at him. That was the trouble with this virus — there was always something new, unknown, that came into play just when everyone thought things were under control.

Jim was torn by worry. He, too, was seropositive, but he was lucky so far. His health was fairly good. Yet, he worried about himself and he worried about Paul, his partner who was so ill. Every little sound that came from Paul either woke him or made him go to the room to see if he was all right. Jim knew that he needed time away. A break would give him new life, new energy. At first, it was hard to take a break every once in a while. But he came to see that he needed time to get himself together. He also knew that Paul, too, needed time free from his constant presence. Love brought them together. Love was keeping them together. Love would eventually bind them even after death.

Love

AIDS made all people rediscover the importance of love in human life. Christian faith centres itself on love, but sometimes it takes a crisis such as this to make one see how central it really is. AIDS has made those affected by it very much aware of love's essential place in their lives as believers.

There is a suffering experienced in living with HIV/AIDS that bonds people deeply. The shared suffering unearths feelings of authentic compassion and delight in the good and beautiful wherever it is found. Yet, more than two people or a small community of people affected are involved. Because they have come to realize that God remains present with them and even suffers with them, humanity and divinity are joined not only in the pain and suffering, but in the concern and delight.

The concern and the delight enable them to become fully alive and to be in a caring relationship with others. In this relationship they not only take care of the other, but are themselves cared for. Together both the helper and the one who is helped delight in whatever thing of beauty they find and experience. When concern and delight are bound together in suffering, as they are in the case of persons affected by AIDS, they create an intensity of human life which cannot be known outside of such an experience. Friends are bound in a love which produces a new emphasis on the life within and between them, a new sensitivity to their spiritual-bodily existence together.

Jesus, the Lover

Love — given and experienced — forms the very heart of who Jesus Christ is and what he taught. "I give you a new commandment: that you love one another. Just as I have loved you, you also should love one another. By this everyone will know that you are my disciples, if you have love for one another" (John 13:34-35). Upon looking through the four Gospels we find narrations about Jesus which involve us and anchor us in the lived reality of Jesus Christ. And, in doing so, we discover that love is not only the heart of Jesus' message — it is the whole message.

Jesus' whole life was an incarnation of care and concern for others. He believed and felt that if one cared for and was concerned with the welfare of other human beings, each and every human being would grow. There would be a world in which all could live freely and in an authentically human way. Jesus felt with the widow whose only son had died (Luke 7:11-17). He raised him. Jesus was overwhelmed with grief at the death of his friend Lazarus (John 11:1-44). Jesus had not been there when Lazarus died and he wept in deep sorrow. Then, he called him forth.

Jesus showed love, not condemnation, for people whom his society judged and condemned. By so doing, Jesus showed the love and passion of God who does not condemn but offers love as a possibility for life. Everywhere the Gospels portray Jesus as one who offers love, concern and compassion in some way or other. What he does not offer is judgement and condemnation. He reminds his disciples they are not to judge others (Matthew 7:1-5). Various Christian denominations which profess to be incarnations of his way more often than not offer exactly the opposite when it comes to HIV and AIDS. Some judge. Some condemn. Perhaps this explains why so many persons living with AIDS move away from organized religion, but not away from Jesus Christ and the love which he maintained was the key to human life.

Love of its very nature moves us into action. Love sees and concerns itself with wholeness — the wholeness of the other and the self at the same time. Love is not a matter of saying, "I will pray for you," then leaving the person in his or her loneliness. When Jesus said, "Not every one who says to me, 'Lord, Lord' will enter the kingdom of heaven, but only the one who does the will of my Father in heaven. . . . Everyone then who hears these words of mine and acts on them will be like a wise man who built his house on rock" (Matthew 7:21-24), he was stressing the need to be committed to him, and to love. Jesus cares nothing for a profession of faith which remains only in the mind and on the lips. Just the opposite. It is not *what* we believe but *in whom* we believe that makes us whole. Dogmatic or moralistic affirmations do not give life, but love lived in commitment to life in Jesus does.

The command to love is the very essence of Jesus' teaching. Love destroys everything that would otherwise make life less than human. As Ron Bergeron said: "In and through love, the darkness can be overcome and the mansion of relation gained. Trusting overcomes distrust, and accepting God's love for each of us is the first and only necessary step into the light of grace." We all exist in some way in an atmosphere of darkness where there is no trust. We look at others and wonder what we can get from them. Or we fear what they might want from us. It is love — authentic care and concern for the other — which removes that shadow side. Love allows us to enter once again into a healthy, whole and life-giving relationship with God and others. Distrust is transformed into trust and we are able to live together.

To live together in this love requires that we dare to receive the love which God has for us and gives us. One must "dare" to receive it because we do not know where it will lead us; hence, we must take the risk of not being in control of our destiny. Whether we are women or men, wealthy or poor, gay or straight, God loves us with an equal and mutual kind of empowering love. In receiving this gift of love, we launch out to whole new ways of living. We move into creative relationships with other people, partners, friends, and even people we barely know. We move into a relationship with the Transcendent, who continuously loves us with a love that is free and liberating. To enter it demands only that we say yes to the love which God gives at every moment. Daring to take the chance — the risk of faith — produces a movement of life-love within us. The gift we receive compels us to be and to live for others. And as Ron said, "Love is not a space to own or to possess. It can only be entered into and shared." In receiving God's love, we open our hearts to the reality of sharing — God's sharing is God's life with us, and our sharing is our life with God . . . and with others.

Love creates life

For God, sharing is creating. God opens up to us and to the world by giving life, hope and beauty. We live and we love because God provides us with the very foundation to existence. God is love and, therefore, the prime element and atmosphere of the spirituality of any believer. Naturally this includes all persons living with AIDS. John the Evangelist reminds us of this when he writes to his community: "Beloved, since God loved us so much, we also ought to love one another. . . . If we love one another, God lives in us and his love is perfected in us" (I John 4:11-12). There is no other way in which God can be seen, known or loved except in and through each one of us. But what is important is that we love, that we open ourselves to life for others. The former Secretary General of the United Nations, Dag Hammarksjold, urged people to dare to be themselves. He wanted them to be authentically who they were, so that they might give life to others.

When we love we create life. To love the beauty of the mountains, the ocean, the flowers and the animals is to create joy within ourselves. Joy always gives us energy and the desire to live. When we love other human beings there is a certain life-giving joy within us. Even more, by opening to others in love, we create that reality in them as well. In all of this, God is alive, creating and re-creating in and through us.

For most people living with AIDS, loving in this way is not easy. All too often they are the objects of hate and even violence. The violence has been vicious at times. In the United States and Canada, people have been attacked and beaten violently simply because they were gay and had AIDS. Sometimes the violence is subtle; for example, being avoided by former friends, being left to wait for a long time in a hospital bed after ringing for help, not being touched by others because of their fear of infection. Yet, it is precisely this difficulty in loving that makes love all the more urgent and necessary. Only love can counter violence. To love in these circumstances is to love with the generosity of God. To love amidst hatred is to witness to the daring of the Gospel.

In real life, we cannot always take up the challenge to love, and that's okay. But when we can love in the midst of oppression and violence — subtle or physical — the darkness is destroyed. When loved, people suffering in the midst of the violence find hope and know that they are not alone. This gives them strength to go on. Little by little, love restores harmony to their lives, and the lives of others. Love creates life even if we do not see it immediately.

The challenge of love

How many times have nurses and doctors changed because of the love they have seen between gay partners who will not abandon each other because of the disease? Often, seeing this love enables health care personnel to move beyond their own homophobia to see human beings living and loving as God-given gifts to each other. It also helps them act like human beings rather than technicians of health who "must" cure the body. AIDS challenges medical professionals to see human beings rather than simply cases or patients.

When parents who have been uncomfortable with their gay son see the love which his gay and lesbian family offers, and which he in turns offers them, they are healed little by little. Often, they become activists to transform the negative attitudes of society and Church towards AIDS and the people who are attacked by it. For they see clearly in the love their son receives and gives that God is there.

The lifestyle of people living with AIDS comes to be centred on loving — themselves, their partners, their caregivers, their friends. I say this to affirm that they are not passive victims who simply suffer everything. To love oneself and others means actively relating with others, and daring to challenge doctors and nurses as well as partners and friends at times. One time Ron met a nurse in the hospital who told him that she couldn't accept his lifestyle and that, as a Christian, she felt she had to tell him to change. He then spent much time challenging her views to help her understand. On another occasion he had to deal with a doctor whose fear of the disease was evident when he came to examine Ron's eyes, which were beginning to weaken because of CMV: the doctor wore a mask and gloves. Ron told him that he did not have to do that. He would not get the virus by examining his eyes. Sometimes persons with AIDS challenge their partners and friends to stop treating them as if they were going to die tomorrow.

At times to love may mean to let go. To love a partner when one is ill may mean telling him or her to take a few days off, or to go somewhere for a holiday and rest. It may mean telling the caregiver that one does not want to be controlled, that one wants to make one's own decisions. When people with AIDS love, they reveal the challenge of God's own unconditional love — a challenge to others to love as God does without judging and hating and punishing. This love is a compassionate feeling with the other and an opening up to the other. Loving as God loves is the foundation of true human solidarity.

Love of self and others

Spirituality is often seen as an escape. It becomes for some a private, "inner" world which has to do only with "me." If spirituality were simply a me-and-God thing, we would be ignoring the communal (human) dimension of life. When we speak of spirituality we refer to a lifestyle which moves us into reality. A me-and-God focus only moves us into the false self of isolation. While prayer, meditation and contemplation are marvellous realities in their own right, they can be truncated if they do not move one to relate to others. Thus, they lose their authentically Christian sense.

People living with AIDS — the ones we speak of in this book and whose experience witnesses to this spirituality — are not those who have fallen back onto themselves. No, they are people whose prayer stems from solidarity with the whole of humanity, whether they are conscious of it or not. Because of this oneness with the human community in Christ, the person takes on the role of helping to create a new world. When people live with AIDS, they come very quickly to what is important in life. Believers with AIDS take their commitment to Christ ever more seriously. Their commitment is to re-create a life-giving world for the whole of humanity. That commitment moves them to offer hope to others. By being who they are as honestly as possible, they become bridge builders for others. By loving and living fully, they give others the chance to see what life and love are. This challenges others to do likewise and so re-create a more loving, life-giving world.

Ron saw every stage of AIDS as a challenge. He often wondered what he would get out of this for himself! More importantly, he also wondered what he could give to others by living this out. He was afraid of what would happen as the disease progressed. One day the doctors told him that the CMV affecting his eyesight would probably affect his brain and cause dementia. Ron, who had always prided himself on his wit and sharp intellect, feared that experience. He gradually reconciled himself to the possibility and even joked about it: "When the doctor told me that I might lose the use of my mental faculties, I wondered how I could live and function. But then, I thought, look at the Prime Minister, he seems to be living without them!" Yet, with all his joking, he nonetheless realized that each step was part of *his* journey to full life, even now. He felt deeply that this was a time of grace for him to learn to live through each stage with all it contained.

In so doing, Ron also lived for others. He and others came to realize that wholeness, or salvation, does not just happen. It is always mediated by the events and people with whom we enter into contact day after day. When I visited him at home in the last few months of his life, he was blind. Yet, he adjusted to blindness by doing all he could to heighten his other senses. He listened to talking books. He would ask me to tell him what the day looked like outside in the garden. Sometimes, before I arrived, he would prepare to play a joke on me, by placing small, rubber spiders near my chair. Once I had sat down, he would ask me to look for something under the chair and then he'd wait to hear my reaction. I don't think he did it purely and simply as a joke. He knew that I was getting somewhat discouraged because of my work and the burden of seeing him so ill. He wanted to make me laugh. Humour was his contribution to my salvation. And, indeed, his own.

People with AIDS and HIV very often investigate what they can do for others. Some become activists and devote much of their time when they are well to promoting AIDS education or working to obtain more funding from governments for research and practical care of persons living with the disease. They want to use whatever time they have to help others.

Each personality has unique gifts to offer for re-creating the world and other people. Sam had just finished his training in therapeutic massage. Though he realized his time was drawing to a close here, he wondered what he could offer. He did not see himself as very gifted. In fact, despite his bravado about his youthful looks, he felt inferior. Then, it dawned on him that he could use massage to comfort other persons with AIDS. So, he volunteered to do this with one of the AIDS organizations. He had received his gift of love and wanted to share part of that with others. There are artists, musicians, actors and writers who are living with AIDS and still creating. They create for themselves certainly — there is an inner need to do so. But they create for others: for the happiness of others who will share their creations of beauty and wonder.

Every person is a gift and has something to share with others, and with the world as a whole. For some, like Sam, it may be using their talents. For others it may be spending time with persons living with AIDS who are alone and want somebody to talk to. It may be consoling people who are newly diagnosed. Or it may be doing some office chores in an AIDS organization to free others to be directly involved with persons living with AIDS. In all these things, the person chooses to share the quality of life which he or she has discovered in the self. As a result of the love offered, the other and the world are made more human.

To do all this, however, persons living with AIDS must look at reality seriously and intensely. This is no simple task. In the face of AIDS, one experiences anger, fear and loss of control. The fear is not so much of dying as of the process of dying. They have seen too many of their friends suffer great pain. There is the anger that their lives, which they had expected to be much longer, now seem cut drastically short. They must struggle to live in spite of all those doctors, pastors and family members who tell them day after day that they will die. They have to see death. Yes. But they have to affirm life and hope in the face of this reality. Yet, as they examine and face life with whatever energy and hope they can muster, they discover something positive, something of the light which is on the path. They discover themselves and who they have been and, therefore, what they can offer now.

Yet, in all this, the people of God living with AIDS must remember something Ron said: "Accepting responsibility for our present, while at the same time being gentle with our past, is a first step in coming to awareness of the fact that living is a two-way street and God directs the traffic." To see who we are and say: "This is me," is a crucial step. Who we are now is who we have been. My story is the total me, past, present and future. Unfortunately, we feel guilt and shame all too often for things of the past — guilt and shame which are needless, but which come because we have internalized the condemnation of society. I must claim my story, but I must live. My story may contain elements of destruction for myself and for others; nonetheless, I claim that story while at the same time recognizing that the compassion and understanding of our God does not hold it against me. This is being gentle with our past. And through the Gospels Jesus says this is not only fine, but the way to imitate our God — we must know who we are and accept that God loves us as we are. Life involves others as well as ourselves. Our lives interconnect and meet. And our God is there loving and living with, in and through us.

We discover this God by looking at those around us and at life's events (both the positive and seemingly negative ones). In these events we discover the wholeness and goodness of God as well as the mysterious presence of darkness which can never permanently overcome the light and the direction of our lives in God. The lifestyle of one committed to Jesus Christ involves daring, risking and incarnating love for everyone.

Persons living with AIDS have shown us time and again that commitment means appreciating the need to concentrate on living each moment with all that it may contain. The pain and suffering are to be lived as well as the joy and delight. AIDS leads people to come face to face with what it means to be limited, temporary: face to face with life . . . and death. Consequently, many try to soak in each and every element of day-to-day life as gift, both the wonderful *and* the painful moments. This is the affirmation that one lives and that somehow God is there with the person. This is the whole insight of impasse or dark night — that despite the apparent emptiness and hopelessness, God is there with us, closer than ever before.

This is not the time for intellectual games which attempt to figure out the problem of evil and its existence in the face of an all-powerful, loving God. There is merely the reality they are living and facing day after day. They *feel* the pain. They see it. They live it. Even pain says, "I'm alive." Medication may alleviate that pain, thus allowing people with AIDS to live life more fully. They live it all, taking in the totality of creation and what it means to be alive and presenting this to those who are with them. Each one does it in one's own way, with whatever possibilities may be in store for them. They are not always thinking about how to do it. There are times when they cannot muster the strength. This is part of it. They simply live and what flows from that is their gift to others.

Persons living with AIDS contribute to the world by creating life for themselves. Everything they have been and create — whether it be love, friendship, beautiful art or whatever — is now part of their life. This is their legacy to all human beings. We all live, and this life is the beginning of eternal life. We all touch the world. We all change it by being who we are, by being and claiming our story. Believers living with AIDS say by their lives that moving out of total self-interest to concern for others creates life for them and for others.

One body — together

All that we have said and all that Christians with AIDS express in their lives lead us to recognize the underlying sense of community. In I Corinthians 12:12, 24-26 we read the familiar text: "For just as the body is one and has many members, and all the members of the body, though many, are one body, so it is with Christ. . . . But God has so arranged the body, giving greater honor to the inferior member, that there may be no dissension with the body, but the members may have the same care for one another. If one member suffers, all suffer together with it; if one member is honored, all rejoice together with it." Christian spirituality is community spirituality. None of us is alone. By our faith we form one community open to each other. By loving we give life to each other. Indeed, this oneness of life is shared with all human beings wherever they live, whatever their culture. We are all human beings loved by God.

The Christian community, or Church, consists of those who believe in Jesus Christ as the one who manifests God and the one who has journeyed the path of human life with us. Our bonds of oneness are vivified by the guiding presence of the Spirit who provides life through and in each of us. That life is love. As community we are committed to each other and to the whole world in a process which is moving towards fullness in Christ. Each of us, individually and in groups, walks different paths. We are unique but concrete incarnations of different gifts in our individual lives. Each of us contributes as we are and who we are to the wellness of the community: gay, straight, coupled, single, with children or childless, educated or uneducated. But though we walk different paths, God loves every one of us and fills the whole community with the qualities which Jesus Christ showed — compassion, concern, understanding, gentleness, faithfulness, hopefulness.

I have highlighted different paths because we incarnate the realities of Jesus in different ways — according to the giftedness that each of us is. We are all gifts of the one God to the whole of creation. Being and becoming more authentically who we are as gifts of God is the challenge and call to us all; however, being that giftedness isn't always easy.

Gays and lesbians, in particular, have experienced judgement and rejection from institutions which call themselves Christian. For this reason many of them prefer to distinguish the church-institution from the church-community. The institution has excluded and continues to exclude gay men and lesbians if they dare to be the giftedness they are as God's creation. But church-community embraces all God's gifts and forms one people. To be embraced as the human beings we are is to be freed. We are on the path to wholeness together. Ron used to love Teilhard de Chardin's comment that "The gates of heaven open for all together or for none at all." All of us are joined on the path of human life which is a journey with our God. None are excluded. We all live this life of community together and this is eternal life.

All of us are part of this one community, this one body of Christ by virtue of our call to life and the gift of faith. All of us are linked together in the love which little by little re-fashions the world into the home of God and re-creates us as an indissoluble body. This bond of human beings together in God is one which no institutional deformation — even within the people of God — can dissolve in any way.

Persons living with AIDS , by daring to love and share life as they are, challenge the institutional Church to recover the Gospel and the spirit of Jesus Christ who forms us as one body. All human beings together create with God a place of mutuality, devotion and love. Persons living with AIDS, and all people who are believers, are bound to each other in that mystery of the sacredness and giftedness of life.

* * *

Further reading

Archdiocese of St. Paul and Minneapolis, AIDS Ministry Program. *For Those We Love: A Spiritual Perspective on* AIDS. 2nd edition. Cleveland, OH: The Pilgrim Press, 1991.

Reed, Paul. *Serenity: Challenging the Fear of* AIDS — *From Despair to Hope.* Berkeley, CA: Celestial Press, 1987.

5

In the beginning

As he spoke about himself in public for the first time, Andy was nervous. But he knew it was the only way he could make others understand what it was like for him to live with HIV. This handsome young man in his early thirties immediately affirmed that he was a gay Catholic man living with HIV. His years of partnership with Don, who had died just a few years earlier of complications due to AIDS, had been a time of growth and love. "Homosexuality," he said, "is not about sexual acts. It is the love of two men or two women for each other." Like all committed partnerships, his and Don's had experienced difficult moments. But love flowed through it. When Don became ill, Andy stayed by his side and cared for him continuously. For several months, this meant making do with two or three hours of sleep a night. Each noise from Don woke him up from his light sleep. But now, Don was gone and Andy decided to *live* with HIV.

He had lost not only Don, but several friends to AIDS. From the first appearance of AIDS in his part of the country, Andy had gradually gone through a process of integration. Although Andy suffered each time there was another loss, he made the loss part of his existence. So when he was tested and diagnosed HIV positive, it was not such a shock to him. He had expected the news and unconsciously had gradually made a kind of peace with it — though every once in a while its horror raised its head in Andy's mind.

He described himself as a spiritual person and his spirituality was evident. There was an integrated wholesomeness about Andy that all could see as they watched and heard him speak of life, his hopes, his dreams and his desire to help others through the disease or to help the uninfected understand, as well as avoid, the virus.

He had the solid support of his mother and family. This was important to him. They stood by him and would do so in the future. He knew this and so he could go on. He also knew that God loved him deeply, as he was. One could see that his life had been marked by growth and commitment to values which enabled him truly to *live* as a fully human being. His new partner also offered support and that meant a great deal to Andy.

Andy was well on the way to the full integration of all that we have spoken of in these reflections. His spirituality was his life and his life was his spirituality — a sense of meaning and commitment to himself, to others and to God.

With time, I hope that all Christians will be gifted with this spirituality that is so deeply rooted in the Gospel which Jesus presented to the human community two thousand years ago — a Gospel of hope, acceptance, love, challenge and commitment. There may be things that some people do not understand or cannot accept. Nonetheless, God values and loves all persons without distinction. All of us are called to love in this way. This is the challenge of the Gospel.

Persons living with AIDS challenge all of us to live in love. May we do just that!

* * *

Further reading

Kirkpatrick, Bill. AIDS: *Sharing the Pain. A Guide for Caregivers.* New York, NY: Pilgrim Press, 1990.

Shelp, Earl E. and Ronald H. Sunderland. AIDS *and the Church: The Second Decade.* Revised edition. Louisville, KY: Westminster/John Knox Press, 1992.

Other
resources

All major North American cities have an AIDS Committee that is a marvellous resource for persons living with this disease as well as for their partners, families and friends.

In Canada, the National AIDS Clearinghouse of the Canadian Public Health Association has a remarkable collection of videos, which may be borrowed, and written materials to consult. This organization is located at 1565 Carling Avenue, Suite 400, Ottawa, Ontario K1Z 8R1. FAX: (613) 725-9826. TEL: (613) 725-3769.

In the United States, the National Catholic AIDS Network sponsors a yearly conference on AIDS. It also serves as a source of contact for Catholic AIDS organizations and individuals involved in AIDS ministries. This organization's mailing address is Box 422984, San Francisco, California 94142. FAX: (707) 874-1433. TEL: (707) 874-3031.

Suggested reading

Memoirs

Ashe, Arthur, and Arnold Rampersand. *Days of Grace: A Memoir.* New York, NY: Alfred A. Knopf, 1983.

Brown, Joe (ed). *A Promise to Remember: The Names Project Book of Letters.* New York, NY: Avon Books, 1992.

Callen, Michael. *Surviving* AIDS. New York, NY: Harper-Collins Publishers, 1990.

Clark, J. Michael. *Diary of a Southern Queen: An* HIV+ *Vision Quest.* Dallas, TX: Monument Press, 1990.

Monette, Paul. *Borrowed Time: An* AIDS *Memoir.* San Diego, CA: Harcourt, Brace, Jovanovich, 1988.

Nungesser, Lon G. *Epidemic of Courage: Facing* AIDS *in America.* New York, NY: St. Martin's Press, 1986.

Peabody, Barbara. *The Screaming Room: A Mother's Journal of Her Son's Struggle with* AIDS — *A True Story of Love, Dedication and Courage.* New York, NY: Avon Books, 1986.

Peavy, Fran. *A Shallow Pool of Time: An* HIV+ *Woman Grapples with the* AIDS *Epidemic.* Philadelphia, PA/Santa Cruz, CA: New Society Publishers, 1990.

Rudd, Andrea, and Darien Taylor. *Positive Women: Voices of Women Living with* AIDS. Toronto, ON: Second Story Press, 1992.

White, Ryan, and Ann Marie Cunningham. *Ryan White: My Own Story.* New York, NY: Signet, 1991.

AIDS and pastoral care

Archdiocese of Saint Paul and Minneapolis, AIDS Ministry Program. *For Those We Love: A Spiritual Perspective on* AIDS. 2nd edition. Cleveland, OH: The Pilgrim Press, 1990.

Clark, J. Michael. "Special Considerations in Pastoral Care of Gay Persons-with-AIDS." *Journal of Pastoral Counseling,* 22, 1 (1987): 32-45.

Christensen, Michael J. *The Samaritan's Imperative: Compassionate Ministry to People Living with* AIDS. Nashville, TN: Abingdon Press, 1991.

McNeil, John. "The Gay Response to AIDS: Becoming a Resurrection People." *The Way,* 289, 4 (1988): 332-341.

Pohl, Mel, Deniston Kay, and Doug Toft. *The Caregivers' Journey: When You Love Someone with* AIDS. Minneapolis, MN: Hazelden, 1990.

Shelp, Earl E., and Ronald H. Sunderland. AIDS *and the Church: The Second Decade.* Revised edition. Louisville, KN: Westminster/John Knox Press, 1992.

INNER JOURNEY SERIES

BROTHER FIRE, SISTER EARTH
The Way of Francis of Assisi
for a Socially Responsible World

Adela DiUbaldo Torchia

Adela Torchia shows us why Saint Francis is still so very important for anyone trying to remain faithful to Christ's gospel today.
ISBN 2-89088-617-4
80 pages, 5.25 x 8.25 inches, $7.95

HEALING THE HEART
Desert Wisdom for a Busy World

Kenneth C. Russel

Author Kenneth C. Russell has us sit symbolically at the feet of John Cassian, one of the Desert Fathers and spiritual master to ask him, as was customary in the desert, for a "word" by which we might guide our lives today.
ISBN 2-89088-618-2
96 pages, 5.25 x 8.25 inches, $7.95

KNOWING THE GOD OF COMPASSION
Spirituality and Persons Living with AIDS

Richard P. Hardy

Author Richard Hardy lets people with AIDS tell their story; and, in so doing, their way of being religious, their way of coming to know the God of compassion, unfurls before you.
ISBN 2-89088-632-8
80 pages, 5.25 x 8.25 inches, $7.95

TO ORDER

Novalis
49 Front Street East, Second Floor, Toronto, ON M5E 1B3
1 -800-387-7164
Toronto area (416) 363-3303
1-416-363-9409